Faith Images 2

Faith Images 2
Clip Art for the Liturgical Year

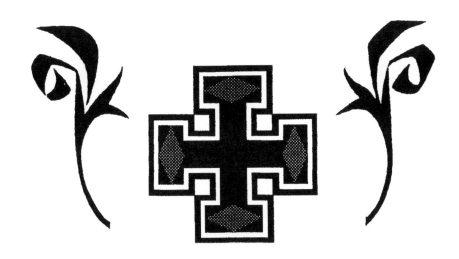

Designs by
Placid Stuckenschneider, O.S.B.

SHEED & WARD

Published by Sheed & Ward, 7373 South Lovers Lane Road
Franklin, Wisconsin 53132
To order, call 1-800-Booklog (1-800-266-5564)

Printed in the United States of America
ISBN 1-58051-049-3

Contents

THE FIRST WEEK OF ADVENT

Behold, the Name of the Lord comes from afar,
and His glory fills the whole world.
—First Vespers

O WISDOM

O ADONAI

ROOT OF JESSE

O KEY OF DAVID

O DAYSPRING

O KING

O EMMANUEL

FEB. 2 CANDLEMAS

EPIPHANY

Christmas

CHRIST'S COMING

SUNDAYS OF PENTECOST

PENTECOST

ASCENSION

Easter

PASSIONTIDE

LENT

SEPTUAGESIMA

SORROW AND JOY

Feast of

CHRISTMAS

LET US COME ADORE

Rejoice IN THE LORD ALWAYS AGAIN I SAY

Rejoice THE LORD IS NEAR

COME
LET US
ADORE

"Come by yourselves
to an out-of-the-way place
and rest a little."

—Today's Gospel

ALLELUIA

HOSANNA

Garden of
Gethsemani

Mount of Olives

Praetorium

Valley of Cedron

HE LIVES

Pilate said to Jesus:

"Are you

the King

of the

Jews?"

—John 18:33

Golgotha

THE **BODY** AND **BLOOD** OF **CHRIST**

Cenacle

Potter's Field

ALLELUIA

He humbled himself, obediently accepting even death, death on a cross!

"Peace
be with you,"

"Take your finger and examine my hands. Put your hand into my side.

Do not persist in your unbelief, but believe!"

ALLELUIA
I AM THE RESURRECTION
AND THE LIFE
EASTER

LU|||IA
ALLÉ
THE JOY OF THE RESUR-RECTION RENEWS THE WHOLE WORLD

ALLELUIA   ALLELUIA

THE
BREAD
THAT
I GIVE
IS MY
FLESH

TAKE AND EAT

"UNLESS YOU EAT THE FLESH OF THE SON OF MAN AND DRINK HIS BLOOD, YOU HAVE NO LIFE IN YOU. THOSE WHO EAT MY FLESH AND DRINK MY BLOOD HAVE ETERNAL LIFE, AND I WILL RAISE THEM UP ON THE LAST DAY."
JOHN 6:53-54

The Body of Christ

YOUR WORD IS A LAMP TO GUIDE MY STEPS.

REMEMBER...

WISDOM
UNDERSTANDING
COUNSEL
FORTITUDE
KNOWLEDGE
PIETY
FEAR OF THE LORD

CHRIST
THE
KING

"The heavens and the earth will pass away, but my words will not."

"FATHER,
hallowed be your name,
your kingdom come.
Give us each day
our daily bread.
Forgive us our sins
for we too forgive all
who do us wrong;
and subject us not
to the trial."

He put a new song in my mouth A song of praise To our God

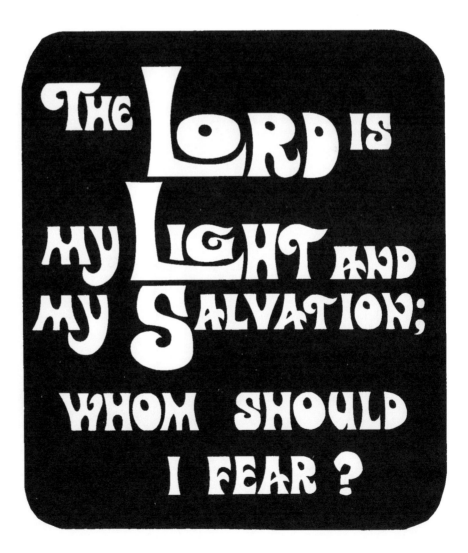

THE LORD IS MY LIGHT AND MY SALVATION; WHOM SHOULD I FEAR?

THEY RECOGNIZED HIM IN THE BREAKING OF THE BREAD.

"I MYSELF AM THE BREAD OF LIFE. NO ONE WHO COMES TO ME SHALL EVER BE HUNGRY, NO ONE WHO BELIEVES IN ME SHALL EVER THIRST."

JOHN 6:35

HOSANNA IN THE HIGHEST

DO THIS IN MEMORY OF ME

Mary said, "I am the maidservant of the Lord.

Let it be done to me as you say."

If I speak with human tongues and angelic as well,
but do not have love,
I am a noisy gong, a clanging cymbal.

LOVE

is patient,
is kind
is not jealous,
does not put on airs,
is not snobbish,
is never rude,
is not self-seeking,

is not prone to anger,
does not brood over injuries,
does not rejoice in what is wrong,
but rejoices with the truth. . . .
LOVE NEVER FAILS.
—1 Corinthians 13

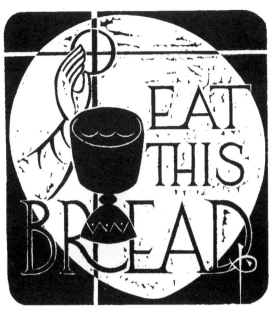

EAT THIS BREAD

O LORD, MY ALLOTTED PORTION AND MY CUP

I am the Living Bread from Heaven

God however, freed him and raised from death's him up bitter pangs, again.

O GIVE THANKS TO THE LORD FOR HE IS GOOD; FOR HIS GREAT LOVE IS WITH OUT END

PRESERVE US UNDER THE SHADOW OF YOUR WINGS

LOVE YOUR ENEMY·

GIVE

& IT SHALL
BE GIVEN
TO YOU

LEND WITHOUT
EXPECTING RE-
PAYMENT

I AM THE LIGHT OF THE WORLD HE WHO FOLLOWS ME WALKS NOT IN DARKNESS

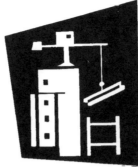

LORD, GIVE SUCCESS TO THE WORK OF OUR HANDS

BLESSED
ARE ...

✚

THE POOR IN SPIRIT ✚
THE MEEK
THEY THAT MOURN
✚ THAT HUNGER
✚
THE MERCIFUL ✚
THE CLEAN OF HEART

THE PEACEMAKERS
✚ THEY THAT SUFFER

The Religious Vows

First Things First

The Benedictine Family

Blessed are
—the poor in spirit;
—they who mourn;
—the meek;
—they who hunger and thirst
   for righteousness;
—the merciful;
—the clean of heart;
—the peacemakers;
—they who are persecuted
   for the sake of righteousness . . .

(Today's gospel)

You shall love the Lord your God with your whole heart, with your whole soul, and with all your mind.

You shall love your neighbor as yourself.

"The peace of the Lord be with you always."